SCHOLASTIC SCIENCE READERS™

LEVEL
1
AGES 5 AND 6

FROM TADPOLE TO FROG

by Kathleen Weidner Zoehfeld

photographs by Dwight Kuhn

SCHOLASTIC REFERENCE

PHOTO CREDITS: All photographs copyright © 2001 by Dwight Kuhn, Dexter, Maine.

There are many different species of frogs in the world. The time it takes for a tadpole
to develop into a frog can be different, depending on the species of frog.
The frog shown in this book is the wood frog.

Library of Congress Cataloging-in-Publication Data available.

ISBN 0-439-31633-2

Book design by Barbara Balch and Kay Petronio
Photo research by Sarah Longacre

10 9 8 7 6 5 4 3 2 1   02 03 04 05 06

Printed in the U.S.A.   23

First trade printing, March 2002

We are grateful to Francie Alexander, reading specialist, and
to Adele M. Brodkin, Ph.D., developmental psychologist, for their
contributions to the development of this series.

Our thanks also to our science consultant Jim Sirch,
Director of Education, Connecticut Audubon Center at Fairfield.

In the spring, you may see
frog eggs in the still water of
a pond.

Each egg is a ball of clear jelly with a small, dark center.

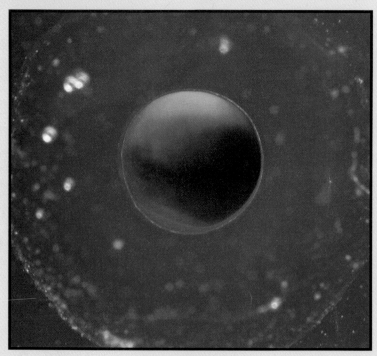

One frog egg

Hundreds of eggs stick together in a clump called frog **spawn**.

Inside the eggs, tiny **tadpoles** are growing.

At first, they look like
small, dark specks.

In a few days, little
heads and tails take shape.

Take a Closer Look

A tadpole inside its clear jelly egg

Soon, the tadpoles are
big enough to wiggle out
of their eggs.

8

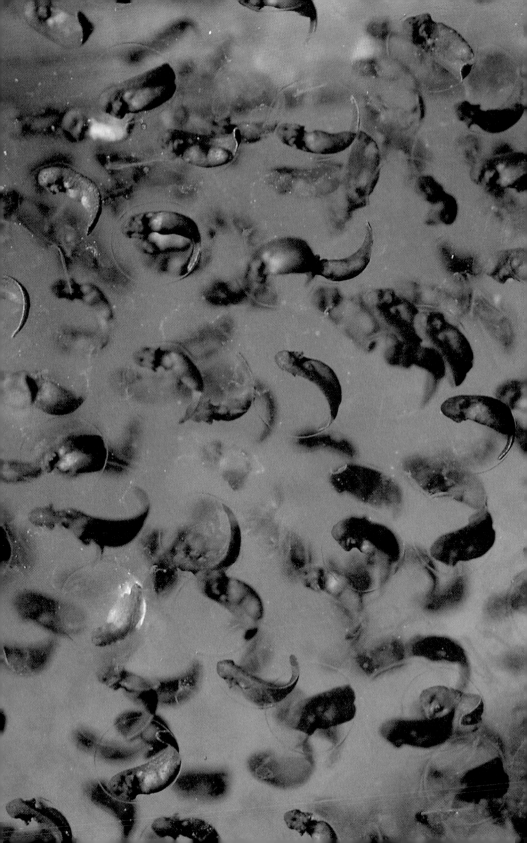

After feeding on the jelly
of their eggs for a while, the
tadpoles wave their tails and
swim away.

Gills on the outside of a tadpole's body help it breathe underwater.

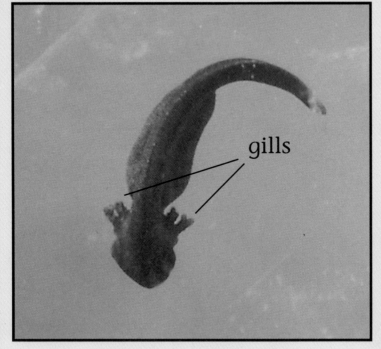

gills

Close-up of a tadpole's gills

The tadpole's main job is to eat and grow.

A water bug attacks a tadpole.

Many of the tadpoles will
be eaten by hungry bugs, fish,
or turtles. But a few escape.
They will grow to be frogs.

Tadpoles do not look much
like the frogs they will become!

A tadpole has a strong tail
for swimming.

The tadpole has a hard
mouth. It uses its mouth to
scrape soft plants from the
rocks and pebbles in the pond.

After a few weeks, the tadpole has grown two **hind legs**. And the tadpole's gills have moved inside its body.

Lungs are beginning to form inside the tadpole's body, too. Now and then, it swims up.

The tadpole puts its head
out of the water. It takes little
breaths of air.

As the tadpole's lungs grow
stronger, its gills shrink away.

Two front legs begin to grow
where its gills once were.

By the time it is about two months old, the tadpole's mouth has become wider.

Close-up of a tadpole's mouth

The tadpole starts
to eat small bugs.

For a few more weeks,
the tadpole's tail shrinks
and shrinks.

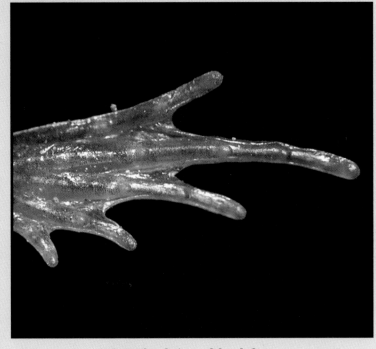

A tadpole's webbed foot

Now the tadpole's strong
legs and its **webbed feet** help
it swim.

The tadpole has changed into a small frog! Soon the little frog will leave the pond.

The frog spends much of its time out of the water. But it likes to stay wet, so it does not go far.

The little frog catches bugs
and worms. It swallows them
in its wide mouth.

The frog eats and grows.
It gets a little bigger every
day.

After about two or three years,
the frog is fully grown.
Every spring, there will be
new frog eggs in the pond.

Glossary

gills—a part of the body most water animals use for breathing

hind legs—the rear or back legs of a four-legged animal

lungs—spongy, bag-like parts of the body found inside the chests of most animals that live on land. Lungs are used for breathing.

spawn—any type of egg that is laid in water

tadpoles—very young frogs or toads

webbed feet—any type of feet with thin, flat folds of skin connecting the toes

A Note to Parents

Learning to read is such an exciting time in a child's life. You may delight in sharing your favorite fairy tales and picture books with your child.

But don't forget the importance of introducing your child to the world of nonfiction. The ability to read and comprehend factual material will be essential to your child in school, and throughout life. The Scholastic Science Readers™ series was created especially with beginning readers in mind. These books, with their clear texts and beautiful photographs, will help you to share the wonders of science with *your* new reader.

Suggested Activity

Help your child explore frogs in the area where you live. Visit a local nature center or library to learn about the kinds of frogs that live near you. Which species is most common in your city? In your state? Keep your eyes open the next time you're on a walk in a park or in the country. How many frogs can you find? If you have family or friends that live outside your area, ask them about the frogs that live near them. If you can't find frogs outside, find frogs online. Visit the San Francisco Exploratorium's Web site all about frogs at **www.exploratorium.edu/frogs/index.html**